WHAT YOUR DOG NEEDS

By Liz Palika

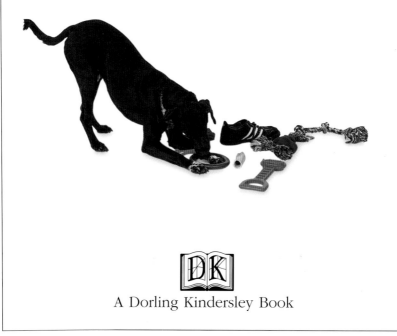

A Dorling Kindersley Book

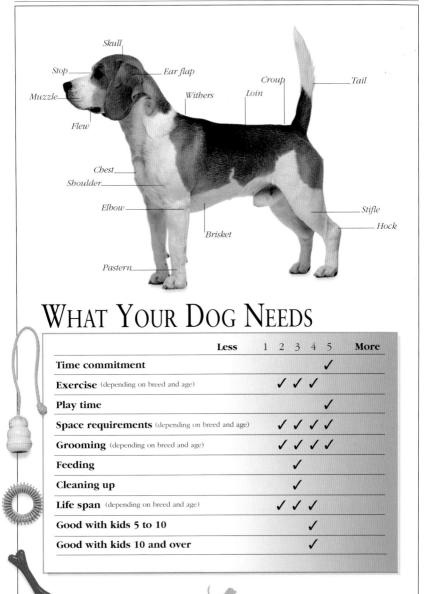

Skull
Stop
Ear flap
Muzzle
Flew
Withers
Loin
Croup
Tail
Chest
Shoulder
Elbow
Brisket
Stifle
Hock
Pastern

WHAT YOUR DOG NEEDS

	Less	1	2	3	4	5	More
Time commitment					✓		
Exercise (depending on breed and age)		✓	✓	✓			
Play time					✓		
Space requirements (depending on breed and age)		✓	✓	✓	✓		
Grooming (depending on breed and age)		✓	✓	✓	✓		
Feeding			✓				
Cleaning up			✓				
Life span (depending on breed and age)		✓	✓	✓			
Good with kids 5 to 10				✓			
Good with kids 10 and over				✓			

CONTENTS

FOREWORD BY BRUCE FOGLE, DVM

So you're getting a dog, or you have one already. Congratulations! Of course, as a longtime dog lover I am hopelessly biased. But if you have been thoughtful with your planning and if luck is on your side, you will soon discover that sharing your home with a canine companion is one of life's very rewarding joys.

We humans are a curious species. Unlike most other living creatures, we have a lifelong need to nurture. This need is stronger in some than in others. My bias is this: For over thirty years I have practiced clinical veterinary medicine and have come to the unsurprising conclusion that pet owners (and people between pets, who don't have one but wish they did) are the most caring people in society – they're the people with an extra need to care for other living things.

We've got another need, as well, and that is to be a part of nature. It is only in the last few seconds of evolutionary time – the last two hundred years – that we have cut ourselves off from the rest of the natural world and became a mostly urban and suburban species. I am

sure that deep in our unconscious we regret the loss of a connection to the natural world around us, and try to fill it as best we can. We bring plants and flowers into our homes. We go camping, visit the seashore, walk in the park...and enjoy living with dogs. That joy is bountiful because it involves reciprocal love and affection.

While these are curious, subliminal reasons why we enjoy canine companionship, there are also practical needs and responsibilities. Not everybody has a working dog, but dogs still work. They herd animals and pull carts and work alongside hunters. They rescue people from collapsed buildings, sniff out drugs and bombs and even the cheese you're not supposed to bring back from your trip abroad. Many of them are working as assistance dogs to deaf, blind, and disabled people. Even more offer their unconditional love in therapy settings, mysteriously and wondrously eliciting responses from people in need that humans could never elicit.

What I like most about dogs is their patent truthfulness. Love, hate, dependency, elation, sadness; all their emotions are worn freely and shared honestly. The best named dog I ever met was Wysiwyg – what you see is what you get.

Dogs enhance life. They inflate your ego, but at the same time remind you of who you are. Dogs see through any pretension, and we all know it. We owe them something in return: To treat them as dogs, amenable wolves in sheep's clothing, not as people in doggy disguise.

We should consider the emotional as well as the physical and environmental needs of dogs. We ask them to live in what is often a crowded, congested human environment, where there are many unnatural challenges and risks; to suppress their natural canine instincts and live with us in a human world. We owe it to them to train and equip them to live in that world. Getting off to the right start is the best preventive medicine I can suggest. This little book helps set you on a proper course toward what I hope will be a fruitful, rewarding relationship with your dog.

CANINE DOMESTICATION

Experts don't agree about when dogs became our companions. Archeologists have found human and canine remains in many different locations all over the world, and for many years it was believed that the ancestors of today's dogs may have joined with us 35,000 years ago. However, archeologists have now found evidence that dates our relationship back as far as 135,000 years. What a long, wonderful history humans and canines have forged!

Our domestic dogs live by many of the same behavior rules as their wolf ancestors.

Experts also disagree about why the wolves, the ancestors of today's dogs, joined forces with us and why our ancestors encouraged them to do so. Wolves, after all, are predators, and a wolf, or a pack of wolves, could pose a serious threat to early humans. However, wolves were also efficient hunters, so perhaps early humans figured out how to use the wolves' hunting abilities to their own advantage. The wolves probably also served as early warning systems, barking if trespassers or predators came near. In return, the wolves were given food from successful hunts, companionship, and protection from the weather.

As dogs became domesticated, their occupations varied. The wolf's ability to find and locate prey was passed down to a variety of different types of hunting dogs. Herding dogs transformed their strong prey drive into an instinct to chase down and round up hoofed animals, including the ancestors of today's cattle and sheep. Other dogs were bred to find and retrieve prey after it had been brought down. By selecting dogs who possessed the skills required for a particular job, as well as the physical characteristics desired, different breeds were developed.

SOCIAL SKILLS

Wolves live in social groups called packs. Each member of the pack fits into a pack hierarchy. A pack usually consists of a male leader (often called the alpha male), a female leader (the alpha female), one or two other adults, a juvenile or two, and the year's pups. Social rules accepted by all of the pack members govern each individual's behavior. For example, only the alpha male and alpha female breed, and all of the wolves work together to care for the pups. These social rules keep the pack living together in harmony.

Today's dogs are able to live well with people because these pack rules are still remembered. True, our families are not wolf packs, but our families are usually led by one or two adults and contain a juvenile or two and perhaps some smaller children. Some of the rules are similar both in the packs and in our families. For example, the adults usually establish the rules of behavior, the adults feed the young, and when the young grow up, they leave the adults. When the dog can recognize some of these (to him) familiar rules, life feels more secure.

However, we (people) are not wolves. In a wolf pack feeding is more ritualized, with the leaders eating first, then subordinates, and with one or more adults bringing food back to the den for the young. In our families eating is more haphazard and with rituals that are unrecognizable (to the dog). Sometimes these differences can confuse dogs, but the uncertainty and miscommunication that arises from that confusion don't have to remain. As you establish a good relationship with your dog and learn what he needs to be happy and secure, much of this confusion will disappear. If you have decided that you would like to add a dog to your family, wonderful! Dogs add much to our lives. However, a dog isn't automatically a wonderful companion. Turning him into your best friend does take some work. And understanding your dog's ancestors will help you both get along much better.

LET'S GO SHOPPING

You will need to go shopping before you bring home your new dog. He'll need some basic supplies so that you can care for him properly.

LEASH AND COLLAR

If you know what size dog you will be bringing home, you can get a leash and collar ahead of time. The leash can be nylon or leather, four to six feet long, with a snap at one end to attach to his collar and a handle at the other end to attach to you. The collar should be the buckle or quick release kind, nylon webbing or leather, and should be big enough to fasten around your dog's neck comfortably.

Nylon buckle collar

Nylon leash

Rolled leather buckle collar

Leather leash

FOOD AND WATER DISHES

These should be easy to clean and large enough to hold as much food and water as your dog will need. Some dogs like to pick up their dishes and throw them around, so for these characters, there are unspillable dishes available that are weighted on the bottom.

LICENSE APPLICATION

All dogs should be licensed, so look into the licensing requirements of your state, county, or city. You can pick up a license application before you bring your dog home.

GROOMING SUPPLIES

These supplies will vary depending upon the type of coat your dog has. A short-haired dog (such as a Doberman Pinscher or a Chihuahua) will need a soft bristle brush and perhaps a flea comb. A long-haired breed (such as an Old English Sheepdog or a Chow Chow) may matt (tangle), and will need an assortment of brushes and combs. A dog with a medium coat (such as an Australian Shepherd or a Border Collie) will need a pin brush, a rake or a slicker brush, and a comb. All dogs will need a nail trimmer for their toenails and something for flea and tick control. Your local groomer or veterinarian, or your dog's breeder, can give you some guidance about what your particular breed may require.

Metal comb *Bristle brush* *Slicker brush*

CRATE

A crate is a travel cage that many dog owners use as a wonderful training tool. This becomes your dog's bed and place of security. Crates come in either heavy-gauge wire or molded plastic. The pet supply store sales people can show you each type; get what will work best for you. Get a crate large enough for your dog (as an adult) to stand up in, turn around, and lie down.

MORE HELP

Dog ownership isn't always easy, even though dogs have been our companions for thousands of years. However, there is a lot of help available to you. Your local book store, pet supply store, or library will have books and videos to help you. You may want to pick up a book about your dog's breed, as well as an additional book or two on caring for and training your dog. You may also want to talk to some of the professionals in your community. A veterinarian, a groomer, and a trainer can all be of assistance to you.

SAFE TOYS FOR YOU & YOUR DOG

By the time they grow up, many adults have forgotten how to play. Owning a dog can remind us, because dogs love to play. In addition, the relationship you develop with your dog is based upon the time you spend with him. When you are throwing the ball for your dog, playing hide and seek around the house, or jogging down a trail through the woods, you are also bonding with your dog and cementing that wonderful, unique relationship that only the two of you will share.

Dog toys must be safe and strong. They shouldn't have sharp edges or little bits that can easily be pulled off and swallowed. They should be tough enough to withstand hard chewing without splintering. In addition, they should be the right size for your dog: not so big that he can't handle it, and not so small that he can easily swallow the toy whole. Some good toys for your dog include:

TENNIS BALLS

Although rumor has it these balls were invented for the game of tennis, in reality they seem to have been manufactured as the perfect dog toy. Tennis balls are easy to throw, bounce wonderfully, and most dogs love them. Dispose of any balls that are getting torn, to make sure your dog doesn't swallow any felt or rubber pieces.

OTHER BALLS

Play only with balls that are safe for your dog. Don't play with golf balls (too hard and too small), wiffle balls (teeth get caught in the holes and they're too easy to chew up), or baseballs (too hard and too easy to chew up). Make sure the ball is small enough for the dog to grab easily, yet large enough so that your dog won't choke on it or swallow it.

CHEW TOYS

Most dogs can safely chew on rawhide bones, but supervise yours just the same. Some dogs will get greedy and try to swallow pieces that are too large and may choke. Hard rubber or nylon bones made specifically for dogs to chew on are usually safe. Do not give your dog bones from the dinner table; they are not safe chew toys!

Chewy bone

KONG TOYS

These toys look like hard rubber snowmen; three balls of different sizes squashed together. When thrown, they bounce in weird directions and make retrieving games more challenging. Kongs are hollow, and when filled with soft cheese, peanut butter or other treats, one Kong can keep a dog occupied and out of trouble for quite a while.

Kong

BUSTER CUBE

This plastic box is also hollow. It has a small hole in one side where you can pour in dry dog food or small treats. Then you can set it so that one treat at a time comes out, or several. As the dog rolls the cube and noses it, treats come out. Dogs figure this game out very quickly. This will also keep a dog occupied for a long time.

Buster cube

SQUEAKY TOYS AND STUFFED TOYS

Nylon tug toy

These toys are great fun, as long as your dog isn't destructive. Some dogs will play with these soft toys, listen to the squeak and really enjoy themselves. Other dogs immediately try to kill the squeaker, and in the process chew up and disembowel the toy. Besides making a mess, this could be dangerous to your dog if he swallows any pieces of the toy.

ROPE TUG TOYS

These toys are fun for two dogs to play with together, or for you to throw as a retrieving toy. However, don't use a rope tug toy to play tug-of-war with your dog; this teaches him to use his strength against you, and that isn't a good lesson for him to learn. Be cautious with this toy if your dog likes to chew things up – don't let him swallow strings chewed off the toy.

Rope tug toy

MAKING YOUR HOUSE & YARD SAFE

Your new dog – whether he is a young puppy or an adult – will not know the rules of your house and yard until you teach him. One of the most important new rules is what is acceptable to play with (and chew on) and what isn't. You can help teach him and keep him safe by dog-proofing your house and yard before you bring your new dog home. You can also eliminate a number of dangers your dog might get into accidentally as he is playing or exploring.

In the kitchen, put all dangerous cleaners and chemicals away, either up high or behind a securely closed cupboard door. Do the same thing in the bathroom, and don't forget medicines, vitamins, lotions, creams, soaps, shampoos, mouthwashes, razors, or anything else that could be dangerous. In the rest of the house, put away (at least temporarily) any valuable knick-knacks or collectibles. You can bring them back out when your puppy is grown up and well-trained. Make sure all electrical cords and telephone cords are tucked away safe and out of sight. Crawl around your house so that you see it at your new dog's eye level. What looks interesting? What looks like it might be fun to chew on? What is unsafe?

Your kitchen is full of hazards for your dog. Make sure all cleaners and chemicals are put away, and sharp or hot items are safely out of reach.

A DOG RUN

If you have a landscaped yard that you're afraid your dog may ruin, or if it's impossible to make your yard dog-safe, build a dog run. A run can be his own space where he can play, sleep, or chew on his toys. You can also teach him to eliminate in his run so that he doesn't ruin your lawn.

• Your dog should not spend all of his time in the run; he needs to spend time with you, too. However, when you can't supervise him or when you're away from the house, the run can be his special place.

• The dog run should be long enough so that he can break into a run, and wide enough so that he can move about. For a medium size dog, twenty feet long by eight feet wide is nice. Larger is fine, of course, but it shouldn't be much smaller.

• The run should be securely fenced and should have shade somewhere all day long, either from a large tree or provided by a tarp or awning. There should be unspillable water, shelter from the weather, and toys to play with. You may even want a radio on in a nearby window playing calm "elevator" music.

In the yard, mend all holes in your fence. Make sure the fence and gate are secure and will keep your new dog inside. Pick up all gardening tools, pool supplies, children's toys, and anything else that could be chewed on or eaten. Make sure all fertilizers, insecticides, pesticides, and herbicides are put away and locked up.

If your dog will have access to the garage, make it safe too. That means all automotive supplies, pool supplies, paints, and other chemicals are up high or are closed in secure cupboards. Laundry soaps and bleaches should be put away. If you store things in the garage, block off those areas so that your new dog won't go exploring in the boxes.

When you're dog-proofing your house and yard, don't assume that your dog will not chew on something. Your dog has no idea that fertilizer could kill him, that antifreeze could poison him, or that the children will be very upset if he chews on their toys. Your dog is chewing to play, to relieve the discomfort of teething, or to amuse himself while he's bored. So protect him and avoid damage by making sure everything is securely put away.

THE HOMECOMING

As you make plans to bring home your new dog, schedule the homecoming so that you can spend some time with him. Many people bring home their dog on a Friday afternoon so they can spend the weekend with the dog, helping him get to know his new family members and his new house. Do not bring him home, drop him off, and then leave again. He will be frightened and may panic, destroying things around your house or yard, or even hurting himself. Instead, plan things so that you have everything you need at home and can stay at home for awhile as your dog gets used to his new situation.

Take the leash and collar with you when you go to pick up your new dog. Keep him leashed at all times once you have him with you. Remember, right now he doesn't know you, and if he tries to run away he probably won't come to you when you call him. The leash will ensure his safety.

Hopefully, you have already bought a crate. If it will fit into your car, use that to control your dog on his ride home. When you use the crate, your new dog won't be bouncing all over the car. If the crate won't fit in your car, have someone ride with you so that you can drive and the other person can restrain the dog using the leash and collar. Tell the dog calmly and gently (but firmly) that he is to be quiet in the car and is not to interfere with the driver!

Once your dog is home, don't let all the family members overwhelm him all at once. Instead, let him get to know people one at a time. Everyone can have a handful of dry dog food or a few treats, and when the dog comes over to investigate, give him a treat or two. Don't play any rough games right now – no wrestling and no tug-of-war. You don't want to frighten your new puppy or dog, and you don't want him to think he should fight you. Instead, keep things calm and quiet.

PREPARE YOUR KIDS

Make sure the children in your family understand that they are to be gentle with the family's new pet. No pulling the dog's tail or ears, no poking the eyes, and no tugging on the whiskers! They also need to learn that if they run the dog will chase them, and if he does he could get overstimulated, jump on the kids, or even bite out of excitement. The kids need to restrain themselves from screaming, as well. That can also get a dog too excited.

Let your new puppy or dog explore his new home at his own pace. However, don't hesitate to limit his freedom. Keep him in the room you're in, so that you can make sure he gets outside when he needs to relieve himself and so that you can interrupt if he begins to chew on something he shouldn't.

INTRODUCING THE CRATE

A crate is a good training tool for your dog, and can also serve as his bed. By confining your dog at night and for short periods during the day while housetraining, the crate uses his instinct to keep his bed clean to help him develop more bowel and bladder control. Even very young puppies will toddle away from their bed to relieve themselves as soon as their legs are strong enough to hold them. While confining your dog, you are also preventing bad habits from being established. For example, your dog will not be chewing on the furniture or your shoes if he is confined when you can't supervise him. We'll talk more about using the crate on upcoming pages, but first let's introduce your dog to the crate.

Start this training during your dog's first day at home, so that he will have a secure place to sleep on his first night. First of all, put the crate where you want it to remain; in your bedroom right next to your bed is a very good place. If your dog is in the same room with you all night, he can hear you and smell you and know you're close by. He won't be lonely (especially while he's getting used to your home), and the time spent close to you, even while you are sleeping, is great for bonding. In addition, if he's close by, you can hear if he needs to go outside to eliminate.

→ Once the crate is placed, prop open the door so it can't close accidentally. <u>Toss a toy, a ball</u>, or a doggy treat inside and encourage your dog to go in after it. If he does, praise him with, "Good dog!" Once he's going in readily, start adding a command, "Rover, go to bed!" and praise him when he does, <u>"Good dog to go to bed!"</u> Do this <u>three or four times in a row</u>, and then stop. Repeat it in an hour or two.

During the next training session, you want to get him used to the door closing after him. Tell him, "Rover, go to bed!" and toss a doggy treat inside. Close the door behind him as you praise him. If he is quiet and calm (as he should be), let him take a nap or set the kitchen timer and let him out in <u>fifteen minutes</u>. If he throws a temper tantrum and barks, whines, and bounces around, do NOT let him out! By letting him out in the midst of a temper tantrum, you are rewarding the bad behavior. Instead, wait until he calms down, then let him out. Do this two or three times during your dog's first day home.

When it's time to go to bed, take your dog to the bedroom and tell him to go to bed as you toss a treat in his crate. Praise him when he goes inside and close the crate door. Go through your own bedtime rituals and turn off the light. If your dog fusses, try to determine whether he's just fussy and getting used to the new situation, or whether he actually has to go outside to relieve himself. If he has to go outside, the fussing will continue and he'll begin to sound quite urgent. Of course, you want to take him outside!

When he goes inside, praise him for being so brave!

Continue using the food treat to encourage your dog to go in the crate for quite a while – months even – so that the crate becomes something good rather than a jail.

Your dog can spend the night in the crate and several short periods during the day. Try not to keep him in the crate any more than three hours at a stretch during the day; he needs time to move around, play, and exercise. If he's crated too much, he may begin to resent the crate and fight it.

Don't leave your dog confined for too many hours, or he may not be getting enough exercise.

Start Housetraining the Very First Day

Teaching your dog to accept the crate is the first step in housetraining. Learning bowel and bladder control by not soiling their bed is an important part of growing up for puppies, and is just important for newly adopted adult dogs, who may need a refresher course in housetraining. All dogs also need to learn where to go to relieve themselves, and a command that means they should try.

Take your dog outside to the place where you want him to go, either a corner of the yard or a special place that won't ruin the landscaping. Be quiet, don't play or interact with him, and let him sniff. When he starts to eliminate, tell him quietly (so you don't interrupt him) "Go potty!" (or whatever command will be comfortable for you to use). When he's done, praise him. Continue taking him outside to this special place every time he needs to go, or as often as you realistically can, for several weeks. He will need to relieve himself when he wakes up, a little while after eating or drinking, and after playtimes. If your dog is a young puppy, he will also need to go out every two hours or so. If your dog is a newly adopted dog with no previous housetraining, keep him on the same schedule as the puppy – every couple of hours. If your dog is newly adopted but was housetrained in his previous home, stick to this schedule for the time being, but he will learn his new routine very quickly.

By going outside with him, you know that he has relieved himself and that it's safe to bring him back inside with you. If you just let him out in the yard alone, you have no idea what he has done or has not done. If you bring you dog inside and he promptly has an accident, it's because you weren't there to monitor him. When you go outside with your dog, you are also there to praise him for relieving himself. This praise rewards his response to your command, "Go potty!" as well as praising him for going in the proper place. Remember to praise him each and every time he does the right thing.

As your dog's housetraining gets better and more reliable, use the "Go potty" command when you are out on walks, so that he learns the backyard is not the only place to go. And as he grows up and learns to respond to the command, you will discover many uses for it. When you take him outside on a freezing cold or wild, rainy night, it's nice to know he will go on command and not keep you outside for too long. When you go to visit someone, you can ask him to relieve himself before you enter your friend's house. And when you stop for breaks on long car trips, your dog will know just what you want him to do.

ACCIDENTS HAPPEN

If your dog has an accident in the house, most likely it was your fault. Either you didn't take him out often enough, you didn't pick up on his body language (circling and sniffing mean he has to go), you haven't kept him on a regular schedule, or you've left him unsupervised. Your dog eliminates because he needs to, and because when he's young he doesn't have much control over these physical functions. It's your job to make sure he gets where he needs to be when he has to go.

In the event of an accident, you can let him know he made a mistake, but ONLY if you catch him in the act. Let him know he made a mistake by saying, "Oh no! Bad dog!" and then take him outside to the right place. However, if you find the puddle or pile

When you're not around to supervise your new dog, put him in his crate where he'll be safe and out of trouble. But don't leave him in there too long.

and he's already left the area, it's too late to scold him. Dogs corrected after the fact seem to think that the act of urination or defecation is what their owner is angry about, and that's not the message you want to send. He has to relieve himself! When he has an accident, it is the *place* that was wrong, not the act itself. So if your dog is having accidents, concentrate on taking him outside more often, staying with him until you can praise him, and then supervising him when he's in the house. If you are too busy to supervise him, put him in his crate or put him outside.

Housetraining is an ongoing process. Young puppies cannot be considered fully and reliably housetrained until eight or nine months of age. If there have been no accidents in weeks, that simply means you have been doing everything right! But even if there have been no accidents, don't assume the dog is one hundred percent reliable; not yet. Give him time to mature, both physically and mentally.

Make time to take him out frequently. Putting him on a regular schedule of meals, exercise, and bathroom breaks will help him develop better control.

GOOD CANINE NUTRITION

Scientists classify dogs as carnivores, which is the same way they classify dogs' wild cousins and ancestors, the wolves. Behaviorally, however, both wolves and dogs are omnivores. Carnivores are meat eaters while omnivores eat just about anything. Wolves and dogs are very opportunistic, eating anything that happens their way. It's not unusual to see dogs sample things growing in your garden. Most dogs will eat strawberries, tomatoes, watermelon, avocados, green beans, and lots more. That is also why dogs will get into the garbage and eat some really awful things – to us. To the dog, those bits of garbage are treasures! But just because your dog will eat a variety of things, as did his ancestors, doesn't mean all those things are good for him.

Good nutrition is made up of several very important components, all of which must be present in the dog's diet. When one or more of these things is missing, your dog's health will suffer.

All commercial dog foods that are labeled "Nutritionally balanced and complete" contain all of the components needed for good health. However, not all dog foods are created equal. To find out what is in your dog's food, read the label carefully. How much protein is listed? Fat? Carbohydrate? Look at the ingredients. How are the ingredients listed? Is the first ingredient meat?

LABELS CAN BE DECEIVING!

Suppose you see a dog food that is labeled "Lamb and Rice." You might assume that the two primary ingredients are lamb meat and rice, correct? You're right, they should be. But that doesn't mean the food contains only lamb and rice. It may have a number of other ingredients, including other meats. In addition, there might be wheat, corn, and other grains. Rarely is a dog food made from just two ingredients. Read the label carefully, especially if you have a dog with a food allergy and you need to avoid some foods or feed a specific diet.

○ **Vitamins** are organic compounds that are necessary for life. They affect the metabolism of food, growth, reproduction, and a thousand other bodily processes.

○ **Minerals** are inorganic compounds, and are just as necessary for life as vitamins. Minerals often work in conjunction with other minerals, vitamins, or other compounds, such as amino acids or enzymes.

○ **Amino acids** are compounds that are needed for growth and healing, as well as other body functions. Amino acids are found in proteins, and, in turn, help the body metabolize proteins.

○ **Proteins** can be complete or incomplete. Complete proteins, found in animal products, contain all of the amino acids necessary for good health. Incomplete proteins, found in plants products, are still good food, but do not contain all of the amino acids needed by your dog's body.

○ **Enzymes** are protein-based chemicals found in every cell in the body. They work to cause biochemical reactions that affect every stage of metabolism. Most enzymes work with a co-enzyme, often a vitamin, to cause the needed reaction.

○ **Fats** help metabolize fat-soluble vitamins, including D, E, and K. Fats also give your dog energy.

○ **Carbohydrates** are sugars and starches, and are used by the body as fuel. Complex carbohydrates (grains, rice, potatoes, and pasta) are intricate conglomerations of glucose (sugar) molecules.

That's good – after all, your dog is primarily a meat eater. All commercial foods have a phone number somewhere on the label where you can contact a company representative. If you have questions about the food, don't hesitate to call and ask.

One thing to keep in mind when you're shopping for dog food: This is one area where you usually do get what you pay for. The cheaper foods are more likely to use cheaper ingredients, including less nutritious cuts of meat, poorer grains, and cheaper additives. The more expensive foods are more likely to use better quality ingredients. What's the difference to your dog? Well, his health for one thing. A dog fed a poorer dog food is more likely to suffer from malnutrition, even if he's eating a lot of food. Your savings in dog food may very well be used up at the veterinarian's office later! Dogs also need less of a premium dog food than they need of a cheaper brand. That's because premium foods have more usable nutrients. When it comes to dog food, what seems like a bargain often isn't.

DOG FOOD CHOICES

Dog food comes in many forms. The most common food is a dry kibble. This food is usually grain-based, with meat and other ingredients included. Dry food is much cheaper than other forms of dog food, keeps a long time in the cupboard, and most dogs eat it readily. The chewing action on the hard kibbles also helps keep the dog's teeth clean.

Canned foods

Canned food is meat-based, with or without other ingredients added. All dogs like canned food – the high moisture and high meat content are attractive – and this can be used to tempt a picky eater. Canned food is very moist, often with eighty percent or more water. It is also more expensive than dry food, especially when comparing actual nutrition. A canned food diet can lead to a great deal of tartar build-up on the dog's teeth, too.

Semi-moist food

Semi-moist foods are higher in moisture content than dry kibble foods, but have less water than canned foods. These foods are often high in sugar and/or salt, so they are often not a good choice.

A diet based on a dry kibble food with a small amount of canned food for taste or temptation is usually a good choice for both the dog and owner. The cost will be reasonable and the dog will enjoy eating.

A wet and dry combination diet

WHEN, WHERE, AND HOW MUCH?

Most young puppies should be fed twice a day, morning and evening. By the time the dog is six to seven months old, he may begin to show preferences for a particular time of day and you can start increasing that meal and decreasing the amount fed in the other meal. Most adult dogs eat one larger meal once a day (for example, in the morning) and have a smaller meal or a snack in the evening. Do not just feed your dog once a day, since a hungry dog is more prone to steal food from the kitchen or raid the trash cans. Most veterinarians also recommend two meals a day.

Feed your dog in a quiet place where he won't be disturbed. Don't try to feed him in the kitchen while you're fixing the family's meal; this is too much activity. If the dog feels his food is being threatened, he may begin guarding it, growling, and perhaps even biting. Other dogs get too distracted by the activity and don't eat well. Instead, feed him where things are quiet and he can relax while he's eating.

How much to feed depends upon many factors, including your dog's age, size, breed, and activity level. Young, rapidly growing, big-breed puppies will need more food than adult, midsize dogs. On the other hand, a small, fast-moving, very energetic dog such as a Yorkshire Terrier may need more food (in proportion) than a quiet, sedate, giant breed such as a Great Dane. All dogs foods will have feeding directions on the label. These will say how much food to feed your dog each day. Begin with this schedule. However, you will then have to adjust the amounts depending upon your dog. If he starts to gain too much weight, cut back on the food. If he loses weight (and shouldn't), increase his food. Watch your dog carefully and base the amount of food you feed upon his health, weight, and activity levels. Your veterinarian can also give you valuable guidance in this area.

SHOULD YOU FEED YOUR DOG PEOPLE FOOD?

As a general rule, you should feed your dog his dog food. Anything you add to that diet can potentially upset the nutritional balance of the food. For example, if the food is balanced with the proper amount of calcium and you add to this diet something high in phosphorus, you can inhibit calcium absorption in your dog's system. This can lead to many different problems, including rickets, slow or poor growth, and poor healing.

Giving your dog people food, especially if you feed him while you are eating, may also lead to behavior problems, including begging or food stealing. Never let your dog hang out under the table while people are eating, and don't let the children sneak the dog food from their plates. What may begin as simple begging can quickly escalate to taking food from the children's hands or plates.

There are times when people food can be of use, though. If you need to medicate your dog, it's much easier to give him a pill if you hide it in a chunk of cheese or a piece of hot dog. So save the people food for those times when it can serve a purpose, and then make sure the food is given in small quantities so that it doesn't unbalance the dog's diet.

Some people foods are good nutrition for your dog and can be used as food supplements. For example, yogurt is often recommended after a dog has completed a course of antibiotics, because antibiotics kill off the good bacteria in the dog's digestive tract as well as the bad bacteria. Yogurt that is made with live active cultures can put the bacteria necessary for food metabolism back into the intestinal tract.

GIVING YOUR DOG TREATS

Treats should be looked at the same way as people food. They are an addition to what your dog is eating and could easily upset the nutritional balance of his food. In addition, many commercial dog treats are very high in sugar and/or salt and are, by themselves, poor nutrition. Too many treats can easily lead to obesity.

However, treats do serve a purpose, especially when you're training your dog. A treat is wonderful motivation! In these instances, choose the best treat you can, nutritionally speaking. Make sure it is low in sugar, salt, and artificial preservatives. Choose a treat that is, in itself, good food for your dog, and then save that treat for special occasions and for training.

SUPPLEMENTS

Supplements are, by definition, something that you add to your dog's food. This could be yogurt, as I mentioned earlier, or it could be a multi-vitamin and mineral tablet. Most dog food manufacturers state that their food is "nutritionally complete" and that supplements are not needed. However, as I've already said, all dog foods are not created equal. A supplement given wisely – so that it doesn't interfere with the nutritional balance of the food – should not adversely affect your dog's health.

SOME SUPPLEMENTS TO CONSIDER INCLUDE:

• A vitamin and mineral supplement should have all of the vitamins and minerals, including calcium and zinc.
• Yogurt is good for digestion, including flatulence. It's also a good source of amino acids.
• Brewers yeast is often recommended for flea control (it's not the best choice for that), but is also good nutrition by itself.
• Chicken broth is good food by itself and can also make dry food more attractive to the dog.

TRAINING YOU & YOUR DOG

Everyone – human and canine – needs to learn the rules of acceptable social behavior. Dog owners must teach their pets not to jump on people, not to bite or mouth people, and to chew on their own toys. When the dog knows the rules and is willing to control his own behavior, he is much more fun to have around; a pleasure instead of a pain in the neck! But training is much more than simply teaching your dog to sit, come, or heel – although these commands are a part of it. Before you even begin training, you need to learn as much as your dog does. Then you and your dog will practice together. This is a cooperative effort.

Dogs are very vocal animals, and because of this, your voice will play an important part in your dog's training. When dogs play together and are happy, their barks, yips, and yelps are high-pitched, but not as high as the yip that means hurt. So when you let your dog know that he's done something right, you will use a higher pitched tone of voice, "Good dog to come!" When your dog was a puppy, if his mother corrected him (for biting her ear, for example) she did so with a deep growl. You can let your dog know he's made a mistake by using a deeper tone of voice than your normal speaking voice, "Oh, no! Don't jump!" Whatever tone you use, your voice won't mean very much unless your timing is good. Let your dog know as he's doing something right, "Good!" and as he's making a mistake, "Oh no!"

Unfortunately, training is not as easy as simply talking to your dog. You also have to make him understand that certain behaviors are important. One of the easiest ways to teach this is to use some food treats during your training. Food treats can be wonderful in helping motivate your dog to cooperate. Choose a special treat that you know your dog likes and use that as both a reward and an incentive. I'll show you how to do this as I talk about training specific commands.

The leash and collar are also important tools for training. With the leash, you can control your dog until he learns the more acceptable behaviors. For example, if he likes to jump on people you can use the leash to restrain him until you teach him to sit. As you begin training, use the leash and collar all the time – even if you are training in the house. With the leash and collar, you have the means of controlling him and his actions. Of course, always take the leash and collar off your dog when you cannot supervise him. You don't want him to get tangled up in the leash and possibly choke himself.

REPETITION, CONSISTENCY, AND COMMITMENT

Training requires repetition. You will have to repeat these training exercises over and over again. After all, your dog doesn't understand why you don't want him to jump on people or chase the neighbor's cat. However, with repetition, training exercises will become habits and your dog will do them automatically. Training also requires consistency. If you want your dog to stop jumping on people, you must stop him each and every time he tries to jump. In addition, all family members should abide by the same rules. If you want the dog off the couch but your teenage son encourages the dog to come up and cuddle, well, the training will not be reliable.

Training your dog also requires a time commitment on your part. Make sure you set aside time every day to train your dog.

TRAINING IS NATURAL

I have heard people say they don't want to train their dog because it's not "natural" for the dog. In fact, the opposite is true! Dogs are pack animals, and all packs have a hierarchy. The lower-ranking members of the pack follow the rules set down by the higher-ranking members. Following the leader is something your dog understands and feels comfortable with. It's the most natural thing in the world.

TEACHING SIT AND STAY

SIT! GOOD DOG!

When your dog is sitting, he's holding still and, hopefully, paying attention to you. When he's sitting, he's not jumping on your guests or knocking his food bowl out of your hand. Sitting still helps teach your dog self-control.

Teaching him to sit is easy. Take a treat in one hand while you hold your dog's leash in the other hand. Keep the leash relatively short (not choking your dog), with just enough to keep him within a few feet of you. Let him sniff the treat and then move it up and back over his head towards his tail as you tell him, "Rover, sit!" As his hips touch the ground, praise him and give him the treat.

If your dog tries to spin around in a circle instead of looking up to follow the treat, you can still teach your dog to sit. Put away the treat. Hold the leash in one hand and have the other hand empty. Tell your dog to sit and gently shape him into the position: Put one hand on his chest and gently push up and back as the other hand tucks his hips under. Praise him when he does sit, even though you're helping him do it.

If he pops up out of the sit position, let him know that was not what you wanted. Say, "No, sit," and help him do it again.

STAY! GOOD DOG!

You want your dog to understand that "stay" means "hold this position." You will use the stay command to have him hold still in both the sit position and the down position.

To start, have your dog sit. Tell him "Rover, stay" as you make a hand signal in front of his face – your open palm held to his nose – and then take one step away. If he moves, tell him, "No, stay," and put him back into position. If he's wiggley, make a soft restraining motion backwards (towards his tail) with the leash as you step away. After a few seconds, go back to him and praise him. Be enthusiastic with your praise, especially if your dog is a wiggle-worm.

As your dog learns this command, you can gradually increase the time and distance you ask him to hold still, but make sure you do so very slowly. If your dog is making a lot of mistakes, you are moving the training along too quickly. Your end results will be much better if you take your time with this training. Advance very gradually, increasing either the distance or the time, but never both at the same time.

YOU CAN AIM TOWARD THESE GOALS FOR SIT AND STAY:

o Days 1, 2, and 3: Take one step away and have your dog hold still for five seconds.

o Days 4, 5, and 6: Take three steps away and have your dog continue to hold still for five seconds.

o Days 7, 8, and 9: Take three steps away and have your dog hold still for ten seconds.

o Days 10, 11, and 12: Take five steps away and have your dog hold still for ten seconds.

o Days 13, 14, and 15: Take five steps away and have your dog hold still for twenty seconds.

TEACHING DOWN AND COME

DOWN! GOOD DOG!

The down is a very useful command, especially when it is combined with the stay. When your dog will lie down and stay, you can have him do so when company comes so he's not pestering your guests. He can lie down and stay when the family is eating so he's not begging under the table. He can also stay while you're talking on the telephone, so that he isn't sneaking off to another room and possibly getting into trouble. In the down position, your dog is comfortable and still, and able to stay for longer periods of time than he can in the sitting position.

Start with your dog in a sit. Show him a treat and let him sniff it. Then, as you tell him, "Sparky, down," move the treat toward his front paws. As his nose follows the treat, your other hand can rest gently on his shoulders. If he hesitates about lying down, a little pressure on his shoulders can help him down. Once he's down, praise him, "Good dog to down!"

If he doesn't seem to understand that his nose should follow the treat down, simply take his front legs and gently pull them forward, laying him down. Don't let him wrestle with you; keep it very gentle.

Once he's down and comfortable and doesn't seem like he's going to pop up, tell him, "Rover, stay." If he pops up, use the leash to restrain him, tell him he made a mistake, "Oh no," and put him back into the down position. Tell him stay again. After a few seconds, praise him for staying, "Good dog! Yeah!" and let him get up.

COME! GOOD DOG!

You want to teach your dog that "come" means he should come directly to you each and every time you call. The easiest (and most fun) way to teach this command is to use a box of dog treats. If you buy your dog treats in a box, you've probably already noticed that he knows what the sound of that box means. When you reach in for a dog treat, he's already sitting at your feet drooling! You can use that response to teach him to come.

Have your dog sit in front of you as you hold the box of treats in one hand. In the other hand, hold a treat that is small and easy for your dog to chew. In a higher than normal tone of voice (happy!) say your dog's name and the word he already knows for treats, such as "Rover, cookie!" as you shake the box of treats and pop a treat in his mouth. Do this three or four times and then stop for awhile. Come back later and do it again. You are making sure your dog is listening and responding to that box of treats. The next day, repeat the exercise, except substitute the word "come" for the word "cookie." Your dog isn't actually responding to the command yet (you have him sitting in front of you, remember), but he is hearing the word "come" and associating it with the shaking box and the treat. Repeat this several times a day for several days.

By the end of the week, repeat the exercise with one important change: call your dog down the hall or across the room. Always praise him with a happy tone of voice and pop a treat in his mouth when he comes to you. By the second week, call him across the backyard, again, using the treats and a high-pitched, happy tone of voice.

Use the box and the treats to practice the come command for as long as you need to. If you have a dog who tends to run away or ignore you, you may want to use the treats for several months so that he learn to do it correctly. If you have a puppy, you may want to use this technique for a year or a year and a half – long enough for your puppy to grow up and mature. Keep in mind this is an important command and the more you practice it – keeping it fun and positive – the better your results will be.

WALKING NICELY ON THE LEASH

If your dog tries to take you for a walk, pulling you down the street, he's risking hurting himself (by damaging his neck and shoulders) and hurting you (injuring your arm or shoulder or pulling you down). In addition, a dog that is always pulling is not fun to walk. However, it isn't difficult to teach a dog to walk nicely on the leash.

With the leash and collar on your dog, have him sit in front of you. Let him smell a really good treat and tell him, "Rover, let's go" as you back away from him. Use the tempting treat to encourage him to follow you as you back up several steps. When he does, praise him, "Good dog!" and give him the treat. When he will follow you several steps at a time, make it more challenging and back up in a zigzag pattern. Again, praise him when he follows you.

After several days (or even a week) of this practice, back away again, but after a few steps turn so you and your dog are walking forward together, side by side. Use the treat to keep his attention on you and praise him when he's walking nicely. Stop, have him sit, praise him and pop the treat in his mouth. Keep this training session very short, very upbeat and positive.

If, while you are walking forward, your dog gets distracted, don't say anything. Just back away from him. If he's not paying attention, let the leash tighten, give it a very quick snap and release correction (the idea is to get his attention, not to hurt him, so be quick but gentle), and when he looks at you in response to that correction, act surprised, "Wow! What was that?" When he follows you again, praise him.

In the beginning, you may have to go back and forth – walking forward and backwards – several times each training session. Do this as often as you need to, but do not let him drag you!

DON'T BE AFRAID TO USE THE TREATS

Some dog owners are concerned about using treats to train their dog, especially for walking on the leash. Don't worry about it! You aren't going to have to hold a treat in front of your dog's nose for the next fourteen years; it's just while you're teaching the dog.

The treat is a motivator that helps your dog learn to do what you want him to do. Later, after your dog is grown up, mature, and well-behaved, you can eliminate the treats. But don't be in a hurry to do so.

USE YOUR TRAINING TO SOLVE PROBLEMS

Basic obedience training is much more than simply teaching your dog to sit, lie down, stay, and walk on a leash. Yes, it does do that, but obedience training can also help you control or eliminate many common behavior problems. Using the simple commands you've already taught your dog, you can shape his behavior in a number of ways. The key is to be creative in these commands. Think about situations where they would be useful. Here are some ideas.

JUMPING ON PEOPLE

Dogs jump up on people to greet them. Puppies greet adult dogs by licking the adult dog's muzzle. Your dog would like to do the same thing to people, so he jumps up. In addition, he jumps on you when you come home because he missed you. He jumps on your neighbors or guests because he's excited and wants some attention. However, if you teach him to sit whenever he wants to be petted, you will eliminate the jumping. After all, he cannot both sit and jump up at the same time. When you come home, or when a guest comes to the door, tell your dog to sit, and no greetings until he does. In the beginning, you will need to control him, either with your hands on him or with the leash, so that he sits still. But he can and will learn it as long as you and other family members are consistent.

Your dog will see any attention – a verbal greeting, a hug, or even a push – as a reward for jumping up. Make sure you reward only acceptable behaviors.

DASHING OUT THE FRONT DOOR OR GATE

This is a very bad habit, because your dog could easily end up out in the street, run over by a car or lost. However, you can control your dog by teaching him to sit and stay at the open door or gate. With the leash on your dog, have him sit inside the closed door or gate. Tell him to stay and then open the door. If he dashes forward, correct him with the leash (a quick snap and release) and with your voice, "Oh, no! Bad!" and put him back where he started. Repeat the exercise. Practice this as often as you need to over several weeks. Train your dog at all doors to the outside, at the gate, and even at the garage door.

BEGGING

This seemingly normal habit usually begins when your dog discovers that people are often messy eaters and drop food. He picks up the dropped food and learns that it's good. He then continues to watch for dropped food, and when food isn't dropped, he begins to pester you for additional handouts. Unfortunately, many dogs escalate their begging, often to the point where they are very annoying, and sometimes even to the point of nipping, snapping, or biting. However, this is another habit that is easy to break as long as family members are consistent. When you are getting ready to sit down to eat, have your dog lie down and stay in a spot away from the table. He can be in a corner of the room or in the doorway, but do not let him remain close to the table or under it. If he gets up from the stay at any time, correct him with the collar and with your voice and take him back to his spot. Have him stay again. You may have to correct him several times at first, but he'll eventually learn!

Basic training also helps control problems in another way: When you train your dog, he clearly understands that you are the leader of his pack. And when it's clear who's the leader, your dog will not be challenging you for the top spot. When everyone in your family applies the house rules consistently, your dog will understand his place in the hierarchy of your family, and you'll all be a lot happier as a pack.

USING CORRECTIONS

How many times have you heard someone say about their dog, "He knows he's been bad because he looks guilty when I get home"? That look isn't guilt (a human emotion that dogs do not experience); the dog is simply anticipating a correction. He has learned that he often gets yelled at when his owner comes home, so his body language is submissive. Dogs live in the moment, and must be corrected the moment they do something wrong. They don't understand the reason for a correction that comes even ten seconds after they've done something. If you want to change your dog's behavior, you must correct him promptly. Your corrections must also be applied consistently and fairly. And always use the lowest possible level of correction. After all, your dog is your best friend! Here are some ways that gentle corrections can be used to solve problems.

BOUNCING ON THE FURNITURE

If you want your dog to stay off the furniture, keep him on a leash for the first few days he's in the house and teach him to lie down and stay at your feet – on the floor! If you walk away and he gets up on the furniture, use the leash (and your voice) to let him know that he's made a mistake. Take him off the furniture and have him lie down on the floor. Tell him to stay and offer him something to chew on so that he's happier to be on the floor.

CHARGING UP OR DOWN THE STAIRS

This is a dangerous habit that could easily cause someone to fall. You want to teach your dog to walk behind you when you go up or down the stairs. Begin with the dog on a leash. As you take your first step up the stairs, tell him "Rover, follow me!" and use the leash to make him walk behind you. If he tries to dash past you, correct him with your voice and with a snap and release of the leash. When he follows you nicely, praise him! Practice this going up and down the stairs.

BARKING

First of all, please remember that it's natural for dogs to bark. A little barking is not a bad thing. But a lot can be annoying. If you yell at your dog to stop barking, you're making lots of noise at the front door – which is the same thing your dog is doing. To your dog, you're barking too! Of course he isn't going to stop

barking, because he thinks you're joining in. In my house we have the Three Bark Rule. When someone comes to the gate or door, the dogs can each respond with three barks. After that, I have trained them to stop.

Start correcting barking in the house when you are close by. Make up a plant mister filled about an eighth of the way with white vinegar and the rest with water (be sure to use mostly water). When someone comes to the door and your dog barks, walk calmly to the dog and tell him "Quiet," firmly but without yelling. Spray the vinegar solution in his direction (but please don't squirt him in the eye!). He will smell the vinegar, stop barking, back off and maybe even sneeze. The instant he stops barking, offer lots of praise, "Good dog to be quiet!"

DESTRUCTIVE CHEWING

All dogs must chew. Your dog needs appropriate chew toys that are just for dogs; if you give him an old shoe to chew on, don't expect him to under-stand that he can't chew on your new shoes. When you catch your dog with something inappropriate in his mouth, tell him to drop it – "Oh no! Drop it!" – using a firm, no-nonsense tone of voice. When he has dropped it, take him to his toys and invite him to take one of those. Or simply offer him his chew toy. Praise him when he picks up his toy. Limit your dog's freedom in the house so that he cannot sneak away to another room to chew on something. Keep him in the same room with you so you can supervise him. And be careful about not leaving things around, especially when you have a new puppy.

WHY EXERCISE IS IMPORTANT

His genetic makeup has given this Golden Retriever a natural desire to fetch and retrieve.

What breed of dog do you have? Or mixture of breeds? Most of the breeds of dogs we keep today as pets were bred to work for humans, and many of those occupations were very strenuous. The dogs had to be athletes and able to work hard, often all day long. Border Collies, Australian Shepherds, Corgis, and Old English Sheepdogs are herding dogs and even today are used to herd sheep and cattle. All of the retrievers, pointers, and spaniels, including Labrador Retrievers, Golden Retrievers, German Shorthaired Pointers and Brittanies, are hard-working hunting dogs. Sighthounds like Irish Wolfhounds and Whippets hunted by chasing down prey, and scenthounds like Beagles and Bloodhounds tracked prey by smell. Rottweilers, Bernese Mountain Dogs and Newfoundlands often pulled wagons, just like horses did. Rottweilers, Great Danes, and Mastiffs patrolled their owners' lands and protected them from trespassers and predators. The jobs that dogs have done for so many years are just as varied as the breeds of dogs themselves.

When these dogs are kept as pets, often these working instincts are wasted and many times the frustration, lack of work, and lack of exercise can cause behavior problems. Your Border Collie may decide to herd the family cats (or kids!) instead. Your Great Dane may begin barking to frighten off trespassers, not realizing or understanding that those trespassers are really your neighbors.

You can alleviate many of these frustrations. First of all, give your dog a job to do. Perhaps he can bring in the morning newspaper. Teach him to help you pick up the children's toys and put them in the toy box. Have him pick up your wet towels in the bathroom and teach him to drop them in the hamper. When your dog has a job to do, he has some mental stimulation and he feels needed – and both of those things are very important to your dog.

Second, practice your training often. Keep his skills sharp and his mind awake. Continue to teach him new things, including a variety of tricks. (I'll talk about trick training a little later.)

Third, make sure he gets enough exercise. That exercise might be a good long walk, a vigorous session of catching the tennis ball, or a run alongside your bicycle. The exercise should be appropriate to your dog's breed, age, and physical condition. Obviously, if your dog has been a couch potato, start slowly and build his fitness. You don't enjoy having sore muscles, and neither does your dog.

Just as exercise is good for your dog's mental health, so is it good for him physically. We people have learned (sometimes the hard way) that exercise is good for us in a variety of ways, and the same applies to our dogs. A physically fit dog will have fewer problems with obesity, arthritis, and other weight-related problems.

Everything about a Bloodhound, from his droopy ears to his wrinkly face to his broad muzzle, is designed to track scent. He needs work to do that takes advantage of his natural talents.

HOW MUCH EXERCISE DOES YOUR DOG NEED?

This chart applies to a healthy, active adult dog. Very young puppies, senior citizens, or dogs with a physical disability may need significantly less exercise or different exercise. (Note that "less exercise" does not mean no exercise at all!)

	Less	1	2	3	4	5	More
Afghan Hound					✓		
Akita			✓				
Australian Shepherd						✓	
Basset Hound		✓					
Beagle				✓			
Bloodhound			✓				
Border Collie						✓	
Boxer					✓		
Bulldog			✓				
Cocker Spaniel					✓		
Collie		✓					
Doberman Pinscher					✓		
German Shepherd Dog						✓	

Cocker Spaniel

Akita

	Less	1	2	3	4	5	More
Golden Retriever			✓				
Great Dane						✓	
Jack Russell Terrier		✓					
Labrador Retriever					✓		
Rottweiler				✓			
Shetland Sheepdog						✓	
Siberian Husky						✓	
Silky Terrier					✓		
Standard Poodle				✓			
Toy and Miniature Poodles				✓			
West Highland White Terrier						✓	
Yorkshire Terrier					✓		

GAMES TO PLAY WITH YOUR DOG

Why do you have a dog? Did you want a friend and companion? One of the best ways to build that friendship is to spend time with your dog. And playing with your dog is a great way to use that time. Play can be as simple as throwing a tennis ball or a Frisbee, or you can teach your dog to play some specific games. What is important to keep in mind is that the games you play can also convey messages to your dog about your relationship. For example, if you play tug-of-war with your dog (letting your dog pull on one end of a toy while you hold the other end), you're teaching him that he can use his strength against you. This is rarely a good idea, especially if there are children in the family. Wrestling is another game that isn't good, because this game also teaches the dog to use his strength against you. Instead, play games that teach the dog to use his brain.

HIDE AND SEEK

Have a family member hold the dog while you call him and then run away and hide. When you first start the game, continue to call so that your dog can find you easily. When he finds you, praise him enthusiastically. When he gets the idea of the game, call him once or twice and then be quiet. Let him search for you. The other family member can tell you if the dog is having a hard time, and if he is, call him again. If you want, the family member holding the dog can tell the dog, "Go find Dad!" or "Go find Sue!" using family members' names, so that the dog learns to identify people by their names. This can come in handy at other times; perhaps you could tell the dog to go find one of the kids, or your spouse.

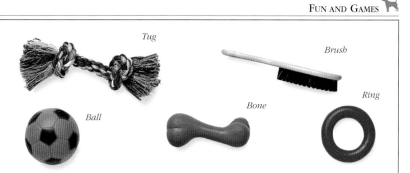

Tug

Brush

Ring

Bone

Ball

NAME THAT TOY

Take one of your dog's favorite toys, three or four different items (such as a bowl, a magazine, and a glove), and some dog treats and sit down on the floor with your dog. Put the different items on the floor in front of both you and your dog. Take the dog's toy and offer it to him, saying the toy's name, "Rover, ball!" If he touches or takes the ball, praise him and give him a treat. Repeat this several times. Then place the ball on the floor near the other items. Tell your dog, "Find the ball!" If he goes to the ball and touches it or picks it up, praise him enthusiastically and give him a treat. Repeat this a few times. Rearrange the items on the floor and place the ball out there again, repeating the exercise. Once your dog can pick out his ball every time on command, change the game by using a different toy. When he can identify that toy, place it on the floor with the other items and the ball. Send your dog after the other toy or the ball. As your dog learns this game, you can continue forever, teaching your dog to identify a number of different objects, including your keys, the television remote control, and anything else you would like him to be able to find.

TEACH YOUR DOG A TRICK

Trick training is just as much fun as playing games. You can have fun with your dog, training him and practicing the tricks, and you can also have fun showing off your dog's skills.

SPIN

Have your dog stand in front of you. With a treat in one hand, tell your dog to spin as you lead him (using the treat in front of his nose) in a small circle in front of you. As he learns the command, you can speed up the circle and increase it so he makes two or three circles per command. However, do not do more than two or three; the idea is not to make your dog dizzy or sick!

Don't try to make your dog spin too fast. Give him time to understand what you want and go at his own pace.

SNEEZE

Have your dog sit in front of you. Gently blow on your dog's nose as you tell him, "Rover, sneeze!" When he sneezes, praise him and give him a treat.

TAKE A BOW (OR SAY YOUR PRAYERS)

With this trick, you will be teaching your dog to assume a position
where his hips are up in the air with his back legs straight, but his
shoulders will be low, with front legs on the floor and head low.
Begin with your dog standing in front of you while you kneel or sit
next to him. Let him sniff a treat in one hand. Take that treat to the
ground in front of your dog (as you did when you were teaching him
the down command) and tell your dog to bow or say his prayers. The
treat will bring his head and shoulders down. At the same time, your
other hand can be under your dog's tummy to keep him from lying
down and keep his hips high. When he assumes the correct position,
praise him. As he learns it, you can stop using the hand under his
tummy and you can ask him to hold his bow longer.

*Bowing is natural for a dog. In dog body
language this is called a play bow. Dogs
bow to one another to solicit play.*

YOUR DOG'S COAT AND NAILS

Your dog cannot groom himself. He relies on you to brush him, get rid of any hair tangles (called matts), clean his ears, and trim his nails. It's up to you to make sure he's clean and healthy.

The easiest way to do this necessary grooming is to set up a regular routine. How often you need to groom your dog depends on how much hair your dog has and what kind. A Chow Chow with a full winter coat will need thorough, daily brushing to keep him clean, healthy, and free of tangles. Rough-coated Collies, Old English Sheepdogs, Irish Setters, Poodles, Maltese, and Springer Spaniels will also need daily brushing and combing to keep them looking their best. Dogs with a medium coat, like Border Collies, Australian Shepherds, and Cavalier King Charles Spaniels, will need combing and brushing several times a week but not necessarily every day. Dogs with a short coat, such as Doberman Pinschers, Rottweilers, Pointers, and Boxers, will need brushing or combing two or three times a week.

If you have a short-haired dog, you can use a soft-bristled brush. Be careful not to use a brush with sharp metal tines or bristles, as these could scratch or cut his skin. Dogs with longer coats can be combed with metal combs, brushes with longer bristles or pins, or a

Slicker brush

Electric trimmer

Pin brush

Bristle brush

Plucking shears

Thinning shears

Scissors

SHORT AND SWEET

When you groom your dog, keep the sessions as positive as possible. After all, you are going to have to do this regularly throughout your dog's life, so make sure it's something you both can tolerate! If your dog is worried about the grooming, have some peanut butter close by. Give him a small spoonful of peanut butter while you're working on him. It will keep his mind off other things.

slicker brush. If you aren't sure exactly what tools to use on your dog, talk to a groomer or the breeder who sold you your dog. They can advise you on the proper tools and how to use them.

To brush your dog, sit on the floor and invite him to lie down in front of you. Begin at his head, moving very gently and carefully. Comb or brush the coat around his ears, using a comb if he has soft, fuzzy hair behind the ears, and then continue combing or brushing down his neck to his shoulders. Continue down his body to his tail and legs. Make sure you have combed or brushed his entire body, including his tummy, under his tail and on his legs. While you brush and comb him, look for grass seeds, burrs, fleas, ticks, and any other problems.

TRIMMING NAILS

Your dog will be relaxed after you brush him, so take advantage of this calm to trim his nails. With your dog lying in front of you, pick up one paw. Separate one toe and push the hair back from it. If your dog has white nails you will be able to see the pink quick inside. Using nail clippers made for dogs, trim the nail so that you do not go down into the quick. That hurts as badly as when you tear your own nail down to the quick. If your dog has black nails, trim off the curved part of the tip of the nail.

If you accidentally cut into the quick, causing it to bleed, scrape a bar of bath soap across the end of the nail. The soap will clog the nail, allowing a clot to form. Keep your dog lying down for several minutes, and next time don't trim the nails quite so short.

If your dog doesn't like having his nails trimmed, you don't have to do all of his nails at the same time. If he's stressed by this, just trim the nails on one paw and stop. Later you can do another paw, and so on, until all the nails have been trimmed.

Nail clipper

THE EARS AND BODY

CLEANING THE EARS

Cleaning your dog's ears should be a regular part of your grooming routine. The ears can attract dirt, grass seeds, and other debris, and regular cleaning can help keep them healthy. In addition, dogs with heavy hanging ears like Basset Hounds, Cocker Spaniels, Springer Spaniels, Labrador Retrievers, and Irish Setters, often do not get enough air circulation in their ears and moisture builds up, sometimes causing (or aiding in the development of) ear infections.

You will need some cotton balls and a cleaning solution. This might be witch hazel or a commercial ear cleaning solution. Dampen a cotton ball and squeeze out the excess moisture. With your dog lying on the floor in front of you, lift one ear flap and gently swab out the ear, getting into all the curves of the ear. Do not try to clean down into the ear canal. When you have finished with one ear, do the other.

If the ears have a lot of debris, a dark discharge or smell bad, take your dog to see the veterinarian. A healthy ear should be just slightly dirty (no more) and may have a damp smell but not a bad odor.

A HANDS-ON EXAM

The easiest way to make sure your dog doesn't have any problems is to use your hands. Once you have finished brushing and combing your dog, have trimmed his nails and cleaned his ears, it's time to give your dog a massage.

Check under your dog's tail as part of the hands-on exam. Look for signs of diarrhea, swelling, redness, or irritation.

While your dog is still relaxed and lying on the floor in front of you, begin massaging him around the ears. Gently palpate the ears near the head; if they are sore or tender, you need to take him in to see the veterinarian. Continue massaging down his neck, feeling for tangles in his coat, lumps or bumps on or under his skin, and ticks. Continue massaging down to the shoulders, down each leg, between each toe and back up to the rib cage.

By going over your dog's entire body this way, you can teach your fingers to know what your dog feels like. It's hard to see what's going on under your dog's hair, especially if he has a full coat. However, your fingers can learn what he feels like. Then, if there is a problem you are going to feel it. Pay attention to any lumps or bumps. They could be bruises that will go away, a tick that needs to be removed, or they could signify a problem that needs to be looked at by your veterinarian. Pay attention to any sore spots. Dogs normally don't yelp or cry during a massage, so if a particular spot appears to be sore, check it out. If there is a cut or scratch, wash it, disinfect it, and watch it over the next few days while it heals. If you can't see anything and the spot appears to be sore, you may want to call your vet and have her check it out.

Give your dog a massage each and every time you groom him. It should be a part of your normal grooming and care routine. By doing this regularly, you'll be able to catch some minor problems before they turn into major ones.

A hands-on daily massage will make both you and your dog feel good. It will also serve as your early warning system for many health problems.

CHECK-UPS AND VACCINATIONS

Your dog should visit the veterinarian as soon as possible after you bring him home. At this first visit, your vet can examine the dog and establish his health status. The vet will look for any obvious problems, including any signs of disease or genetic health defects, such as hip dysplasia or cataracts. If, during the exam, the vet does find a problem, he can advise you on to how to deal with it.

The veterinarian will also ask you what vaccinations your dog has already received (if any), and will set up a schedule of needed vaccines.

The vaccinations given most often include:

- ○ Distemper
- ○ Hepatitis
- ○ Leptospirosis
- ○ Coronavirus
- ○ Parvovirus

- ○ Adenovirus
- ○ Parainfluenza
- ○ Bordetella
- ○ Lyme Disease
- ○ Rabies

Not all dogs need all these vaccines. That's because some areas of the country have a higher prevalence of certain diseases, and because dogs in urban areas face different risks than do dogs in the country. Your veterinarian will know what vaccines your dog needs.

A sample vaccination schedule for a puppy might look like this:

8 WEEKS:

Distemper, hepatitis, leptospirosis, parainfluenza, parvovirus, and Lyme disease

10 TO 11 WEEKS:

Distemper, hepatitis, leptospirosis, parainfluenza, parvovirus, and bordetella

13 TO 15 WEEKS:

Distemper, hepatitis, leptospirosis, parainfluenza, parvovirus, and Lyme disease

16 TO 18 WEEKS:

Rabies and bordetella

ADULT DOG:

Boosters are given one to three years after the previous vaccinations, unless your veterinarian recommends otherwise

ANNUAL CHECK-UPS

When you bring your dog in each year for booster vaccinations, your vet can also examine your dog. He or she will look at your dog's teeth to see how well you are keeping them clean and whether any dental work is needed. The vet will check your dog's eyes and ears, looking for any obvious problems. He or she will feel your dog all over, checking for lumps or bumps that might signify potential problems. Most of the time nothing will be wrong at all, but it's much better to find a problem early during an exam than later, when your dog's health might suffer.

While examining your dog, your vet can also answer your questions. Do you need some help dealing with fleas? There are quite a few new products that make eliminating fleas much easier, and your vet can help you decide which options would work best for your dog. Are you worried about heartworm? This deadly parasite is spreading, and is now found in many areas of the country where it has never before been seen. Your vet can explain how some of the heartworm preventive medications work.

Don't be afraid to ask your veterinarian questions about your dog's care and health. The more questions you ask and the more knowledgeable you are, the better care you can give your dog.

New flea control products attack the flea's reproduction cycle without exposing your dog (or your family) to toxins.

SIGNS OF HEALTH

All healthy dogs share some common characteristics, although they may vary slightly from dog to dog or breed to breed. What is most important is to learn what is normal for your dog. Then you will notice when things are not quite right, and will be ready to take action.

- **EYES:** Bright and shiny, no discharge and no cloudiness.
- **EARS:** Clean with a damp but inoffensive smell.
- **NOSE:** Damp and slightly cool. A slight clear discharge is normal.
- **RESPIRATION:** Breath should smell okay, and should move in and out cleanly.
- **TEETH AND GUMS:** Clean teeth with no (or very little) tartar. Gums should be tight to the teeth and pink.
- **SKIN:** Clean and clear.
- **COAT:** Clean, shiny, and healthy. Shedding should be reasonable, depending upon the season and the breed.
- **PAWS:** Warm, dry and clean. Nails should be well trimmed.
- **URINATION AND DEFECATION:** No difficulty urinating or defecating, urine clear, feces solid and formed.
- **ATTITUDE:** Willing to do things, able to learn, watchful, alert.
- **ENERGY LEVEL:** Ready to go, ready to play (of course, this will depend upon the dog's breed and age).

Your dog should be robust and playful, and ready to go. A couple of lazy days are nothing to worry about, but a marked difference in his energy level could indicate a problem.

SIGNS OF ILLNESS

Pay attention to any of these signs of illness and don't be afraid to call your veterinarian. If you see any other signs that are not on this list but are different from what is normal for your dog, again, don't hesitate to call your vet.

- **EYES:** Discharge, matter, crusty, cloudiness.
- **EARS:** Dark wax, discharge, cheesy or yeasty smell.
- **NOSE:** Dry and chapped, hot. Opaque discharge; green, brown or darker discharge.
- **RESPIRATION:** Breathing heavily, panting, wheezing, unable to catch his breath. Sounds of fluid in the lungs.
- **TEETH:** Tartar buildup, bleeding gums, red or inflamed gums, bad breath.
- **SKIN:** Redness, rash, flaking or itching skin, chewed spots.
- **COAT:** Excessive shedding; dry, dull coat; bare spots.
- **PAWS::** Redness, excessive licking of the paws, heat in the paws, broken nails, nails that are too long.
- **URINATION AND DEFECATION:** Any change from normal, any pain or hesitation during either urination or defecation, blood or cloudiness in urine, soft feces, blood in feces, diarrhea.
- **ATTITUDE:** A change in attitude, excessive sleepiness, lack of caring.
- **ENERGY LEVEL:** A change in energy levels with no explained reason. Hyperactivity, inability to control himself, total lack of energy, inability or lack of desire to do his favorite things.

Periodontal disease is one of the most common problems seen by veterinarians. It can lead to infections, abscesses, lost teeth, and difficulty eating. If your dog's teeth have built up a lot of plaque, a professional cleaning may be required. Dental problems can lead to even bigger health problems, so get them taken care of.

WHEN DOES YOUR DOG NEED TO GO TO THE VET?

MAKE AN APPOINTMENT

Make an appointment to take your dog to the veterinarian as soon as possible if you see any of the following signs in your dog.

▶ **SIGNS OF ILLNESS:** Your dog is displaying any of the signs of illness listed on page 55.
▶ **INJURIES:** Your dog has injured himself and is still limping an hour after the injury.
▶ **SWELLING:** Your dog has an unexplained swelling.
▶ **INSECT STING OR BITE, OR ANIMAL BITE:** Your dog was stung by a scorpion or bit by an opossum or other animal, including other dogs.

GO RIGHT AWAY

Take your dog to the vet right away (call first so they are expecting you) if any of the things listed below happen. If your vet's office isn't open, take your dog to an emergency animal clinic. It can't wait!

▶ **RESPIRATORY DISTRESS:** Your dog is having trouble breathing or is choking.
▶ **BLEEDING:** Your dog has been injured and is bleeding.
▶ **INSECT STING OR BITE, OR ANIMAL BITE:** Your dog has been bitten or stung and is swelling or appears to be going into shock.
▶ **SNAKE BITE:** Your dog has been bitten by a wild snake. Try to identify the snake, if possible.
▶ **POISONS:** Your dog has touched, been exposed to, or has eaten a poison.
▶ **BURNS:** Your dog has been burned, either by exposure to heat or caustic chemicals.

YOUR CANINE FIRST AID KIT

❒ Rolls of gauze or fabric of different widths

❒ Gauze pads of different sizes

❒ Rolls of tape

❒ Elastic to wrap around bandages

❒ Antiseptic cleaning wipes

❒ Alcohol prep pads

❒ Bactine

❒ Bacitracin ointment

❒ Benadryl tablets

❒ Kaopectate tablets or liquid

❒ Hydrogen peroxide

❒ Saline eye wash

❒ Tweezers

❒ Scissors

❒ Disposable razors

❒ Dog nail clippers

❒ Comb and brush

❒ Extra leash and collar

❒ Soft cloth muzzle

If you think your dog needs to see the vet, he does. You know what's normal for your pet, and you are best able to sense when something may not be quite right.

EMERGENCY FIRST AID

If your dog is injured or is suddenly ill, sometimes the small things you do before getting him to the veterinarian can make the biggest difference.

CPR

Canine CPR is a combination of cardiac massage and assisted breathing.

▶ Check to see if there is a heartbeat.
▶ Check to see if the dog is breathing.
If there is a heartbeat and breathing, do NOT do CPR! If there is a heartbeat but no breathing, assist with breathing only!
▶ If there is no breath, clear the airway.
▶ Pull the tongue out to the side, close the mouth, and pull the lips over the teeth.
▶ Inhale a deep breath and exhale into the dog's nose. Watch to make sure the chest rises.
▶ Repeat every ten seconds for big dogs and more often for smaller dogs.
▶ After ten breaths, do five chest compressions. With the dog on his side, place both hands over the dog's heart and push down in short bursts. Do NOT break the dog's ribs!
▶ Do ten breaths, then five chest compressions, and repeat.

MUZZLE

Dogs who are hurt may bite out of pain and fear – even normally gentle dogs. Even your own dog may bite. If you have to move any injured dog, muzzle the dog to protect yourself.

▶ Take a leash, a leg of pantyhose, a piece of gauze, a scarf, or other material and wrap it quickly around the dog's muzzle at least twice.
▶ Bring the ends under the dog's chin, pull them behind the dog's ears, and tie them off securely.
▶ Watch the dog to make sure he can breathe.

SPLINT

A broken leg can be very painful and traumatic. Do not move the dog until you can put together a makeshift splint.

▶ Find something rigid – a stick, a ruler, a piece of lumber, even rolled newspapers – that are longer than the dog's broken leg.
▶ Using gauze, gently strap the leg to the splint. Do not attempt to straighten the leg; let the vet do that.

BLEEDING

Bleeding can be life-threatening. Try to control bleeding before you take the dog to the hospital or clinic.

▶ If a wound is oozing, use a gauze pad to put pressure on the wound until you arrive at the vet's office.
▶ If the wound is oozing continuously, put pressure on the wound with a towel or several gauze pads and consider it an emergency; get to the vet's office right away.
▶ If the wound is spurting, a blood vessel has been broken and your dog could bleed to death. Use a length of gauze or a shoelace to make a tourniquet above the wound, that is, between the wound and the heart. Wrap the gauze around the limb and tie it. Insert a small stick or a pencil under the gauze, then twist the stick so that the tourniquet tightens and the bleeding slows. Get your dog to the vet immediately. If it takes longer than ten minutes to get to the vet, loosen the tourniquet every ten minutes to allow circulation back to the limb. A tourniquet can do more harm than good to a limb, so use it only if you're sure a large vessel has been cut and your dog is in danger of bleeding to death.

CARRYING AN INJURED DOG

If your dog has been injured or is hurt, make sure you don't hurt him any more by carrying him improperly.

▶ Find a piece of wood (such as a piece of plywood or an old door) or several layers of cardboard that are longer and wider than your dog. If you can't find something rigid, use a blanket or sheet.
▶ Lay the board on the ground next to your dog and gently slide him onto the board.
▶ Two people (one at each end) should carry the dog.
▶ To place your dog in the car, slide the board in, keeping him on it.

LOVE AND AFFECTION

People and dogs get along so well because we are both social creatures; we are not happy alone. Many studies have shown that people who own pets live longer, recover more quickly from injuries or illnesses, and have a more positive outlook on life. A more recent study showed that people who own a dog recuperate more quickly and live longer after a heart attack than those who don't own pets.

Dog owners have always known that dogs improve our quality of life. A dog owner doesn't have to go home to an empty house; there is a friend there with a wagging tail, happy to greet them. A dog owner always has a friend willing to go for a walk, even on a cloudy or blustery day. A dog owner has a friend to cuddle on cold nights, a buddy to talk to when times are hard, a playmate to laugh with when times are good, and a companion to wash away the tears when they flow. A dog owner is never alone.

Just as we treasure the companionship of our dogs, so our dogs treasure their time with us. Our dogs don't require much of us; they just ask for our time and our company. In addition to the special time you set aside just for your dog, see how your dog can fit into the other activities in your life. Take your dog with you when you're going places and doing things. Take your dog with you when you go to the hardware store or the pet supply shop. Let your dog help you rake the leaves in the front yard or let him watch you repair the leaking pipe under the sink. As I write this, I have three dogs in my office with me. They are napping, happy to be close to me and waiting for me to be done.

Dogs are pack animals, and they need company. They cannot thrive alone.

MORE TO LEARN

BOOKS

ASPCA Complete Dog Training Manual, by Bruce Fogle, DVM, Dorling Kindersley Publishing
The Consumer's Guide to Dog Food, by Liz Palika, Howell Book House
The Dog Owner's Home Veterinary Handbook, 3rd Edition, by James Giffin, MD, and Liisa Carlson, DVM, Howell Book House
Dog Training in Ten Minutes, by Carol Lea Benjamin, Howell Book House
Natural Dog Care, by Bruce Fogle, DVM, Dorling Kindersley Publishing

MAGAZINES

Dog Fancy • P.O. Box 6050
Mission Viejo, CA 92690
www.animalnetwork.com

Dog World • P.O. Box 6500
Chicago, IL 60680

ASSOCIATIONS

American Kennel Club
5580 Centerview Drive
Raleigh, NC 27606
(919) 233-9767 • www. akc.org

Association of Pet Dog Trainers
P.O. Box 385
Davis, CA 95617
(800) PET-DOGS • www.apdt.com

Canadian Kennel Club
89 Skyway Avenue, Suite 100
Etobicoke, Ontario M9W 6R4
(416) 675 5511 • www.ckc.ca

National Association of Dog Obedience Instructors
729 Grapevine Highway, Suite 369
Hurst, TX 76054 • www.nadoi.org

WEB SITES

Alternative Veterinary Medicine
www.altvetmed.com

American Animal Hospital Association
www.healthypet.com

American Veterinary Medical Association • ww.avma.org/care4pets

Dog Owners Guide
www.canismajor.com/dog/

Dog Play
www.dog-play.com

PogoPet
www.pogopet.com

VIDEOS

Puppy Training 101, hosted by Liz Palika, Alpha Video Productions
(760) 727-8388
www.lizpalika.com

ABOUT THE AUTHOR

Liz Palika and her husband Paul share their home with three Australian Shepherds, Dax, Kes, and Riker. Liz has been teaching dog obedience classes for dogs and their families for more than twenty-five years in San Diego's North County. The Palikas and their dogs like to do things together. Dax, Kes, and Riker have competed in obedience trials, herded sheep, pulled wagons, caught Frisbees, and participated in agility. Most important, all three dogs are certified therapy dogs and regularly visit people in nursing homes, hospitals, Alzheimer's care facilities, and day care centers. Liz is an award-winning writer and is the author of more than twenty-five books, all on pets.

INDEX

Dorling DK Kindersley

LONDON, NEW YORK, SYDNEY, DELHI, PARIS,
MUNICH, JOHANNESBURG

Project Editor: Beth Adelman
Design: Carol Wells
Cover Design: Gus Yoo
Photo Research: Mark Dennis
Index: Nanette Cardon

Photo Credits: Paul Bricknell, Jane Burton, Dave King, Tracy Morgan,
Stephen Oliver, Tim Ridley, Jerry Young

First American Edition, 2000
2 4 6 8 10 9 7 5 3 1

Published in the United States by
Dorling Kindersley Publishing, Inc. 95 Madison Avenue New York, New York 10016

Dorling Kindersley Publishing, Inc. offers special discounts for bulk purchases for sales promotions
or premiums. Specific, large-quantity needs can be met with special editions, including
personalized covers, excerpts of existing guides, and corporate imprints. For more information,
contact Special Markets Department, Dorling Kindersley Publishing, Inc.,
95 Madison Avenue, New York, NY 10016 Fax: (800) 600-9098.

Color reproduction by Colourscan, Singapore
Printed in Hong Kong by Wing King Tong

Library of Congress Cataloging-in-Publication Data
Palika, Liz, 1954-
  What your dog needs / Liz Palika.-- 1st American ed.
    p. cm. -- (What your pet needs)
Includes index.
  ISBN 0-7894-6307-5 1. Dogs. I. Title. II. Series.
  SF427 .P19 2000
  636.7'0887--dc21
00-008259

See our complete catalog at
www.dk.com